WHAT CAN I BE?

★ Career Ideas for Kids ★

"If you don't see it, you can't be it."

Dear Parents,

Did you know that many of the most successful people in the world decided at a very early age what they would be as adults? Usually, their decision came after they were exposed to an image that captured their imagination.

Perhaps the best example of the power of early exposure to careers is Nicole Malachowski. As as five-year-old girl, she saw Thunderbird jets at an air show. She turned to her father and informed him that she was going to be a Thunderbird pilot one day — and sure enough, little Nicole went on to make history as the first female Thunderbird pilot.

Likewise, golf champion Jason Day, music legend Elton John, comedian Steve Harvey, and Emmy Award winner Claire Danes all chose their future careers at age five to ten. Clearly, children can understand and develop a love for specific career paths surprisingly early in life.

Knowing that positive images can inspire the passion of a lifetime led me to create the *Career Exploration for Children* book series. While big words like "paleontologist" are obviously beyond the reading level of little ones, the engaging pictures of children shown in careers in air, space, engineering, science, programming, and robotics can plant seeds that last a lifetime.

With that realization in mind, *What Can I Be?* was created to:

- Provide an early introduction to career education
- Expose boys and girls to a wide range of possible future careers
- Simplify complex occupations so that children can understand them
- Help children appreciate that they can be anything they want

My hope is that the *Career Exploration for Children* book series will entertain, educate and inspire your special little ones to recognize, pursue and live the life of their dreams.

Annie Barron

WHAT CAN I BE?

★ Career Ideas for Kids ★

* CAREER EXPLORATION FOR CHILDREN *

Written and Illustrated By Annie Barron

ANNIE BARRON STUDIO

Every boy or girl wonders...
What will I be when I grow up?

1

What CAN I be?

You can be anything!

scientist

marine biologist

Animator

ARCHITECT

inventor

Let's explore a few ideas...

Aquarium vet

Paleontologist

4

ANIMATE ART

MOVIE ANIMATOR

You could animate drawings for movies. Make your shark a movie star!

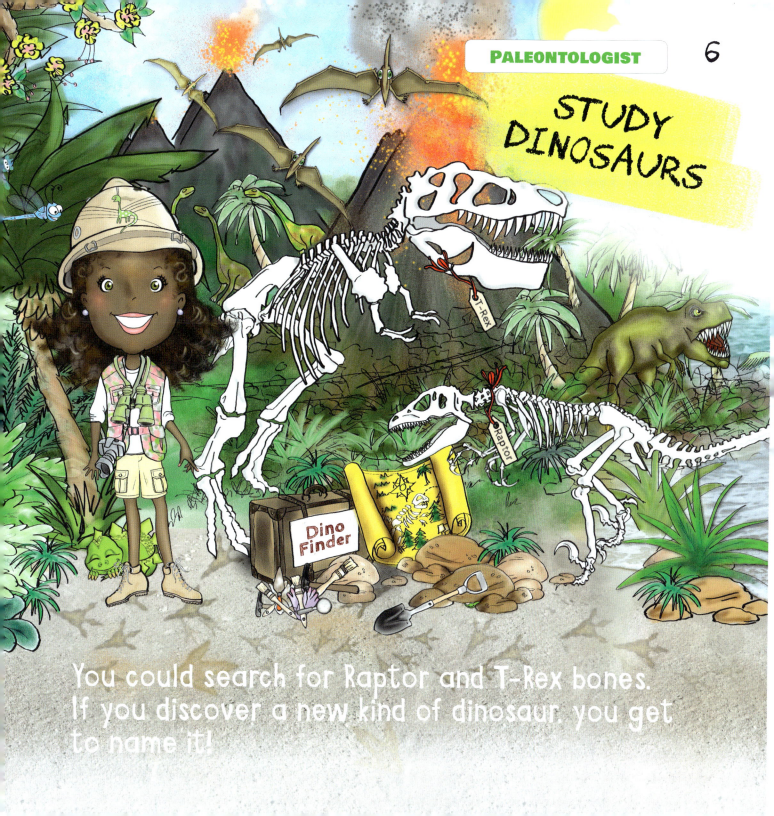

STUDY DINOSAURS

Dino Finder

T-Rex

Raptor

You could search for Raptor and T-Rex bones. If you discover a new kind of dinosaur, you get to name it!

You could study how whales, dolphins, sharks and other sea life behave. What do they do all day?

STUDY SEA LIFE

MARINE BIOLOGIST

Computer Game Ideas

SHARK AND DRAGON BATTLE

Crazy hair game

SPACE RACE GAME

Dino chase game

ZOO GAME

CREATE GAMES

GAME PROGRAMMER

You could make computer games that kids love to play. What games would you make?

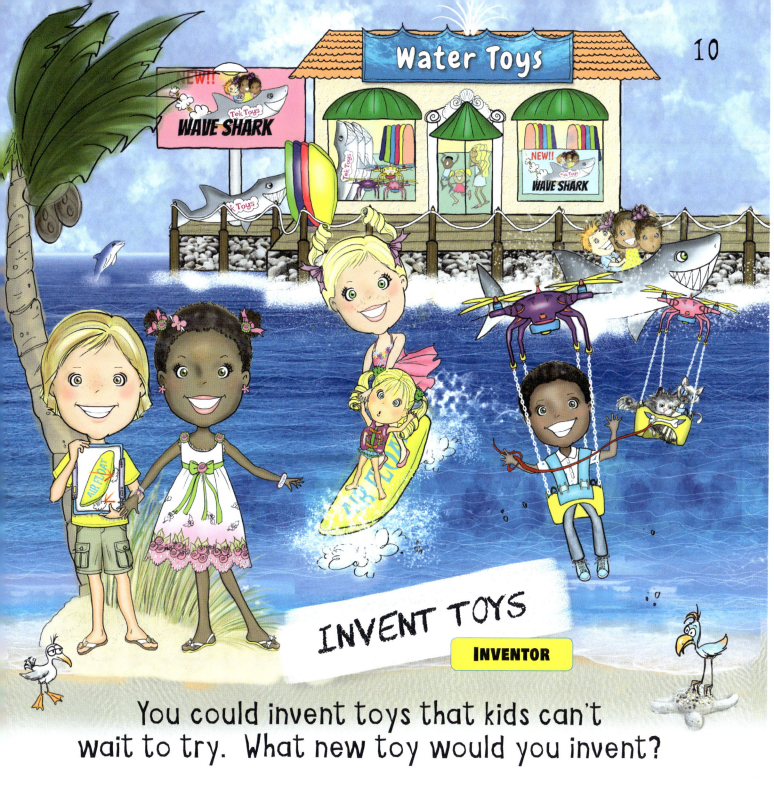

INVENT TOYS

INVENTOR

You could invent toys that kids can't wait to try. What new toy would you invent?

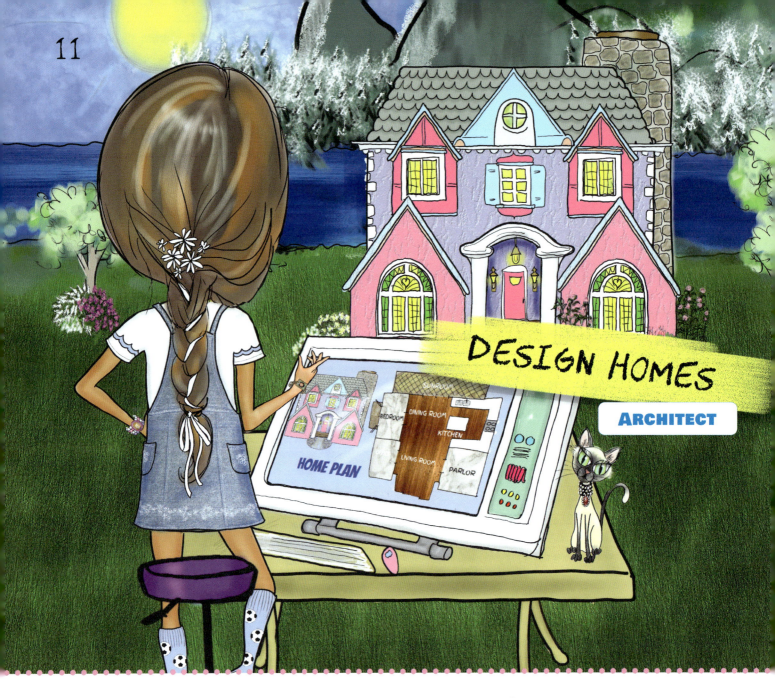

You could draw plans for new homes. Your blueprint tells a builder how the house will look.

You could be a school teacher who helps children learn. What grade would you want to teach?

You could be a vet. That's an animal doctor who cares for pets when they are sick or hurt.

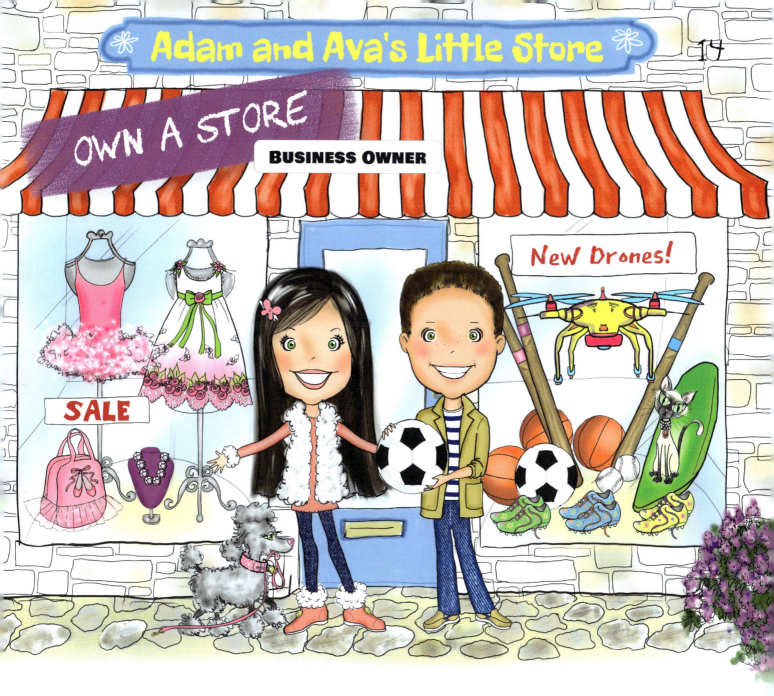

You could own a store that shoppers love.
What would you sell in your shop?

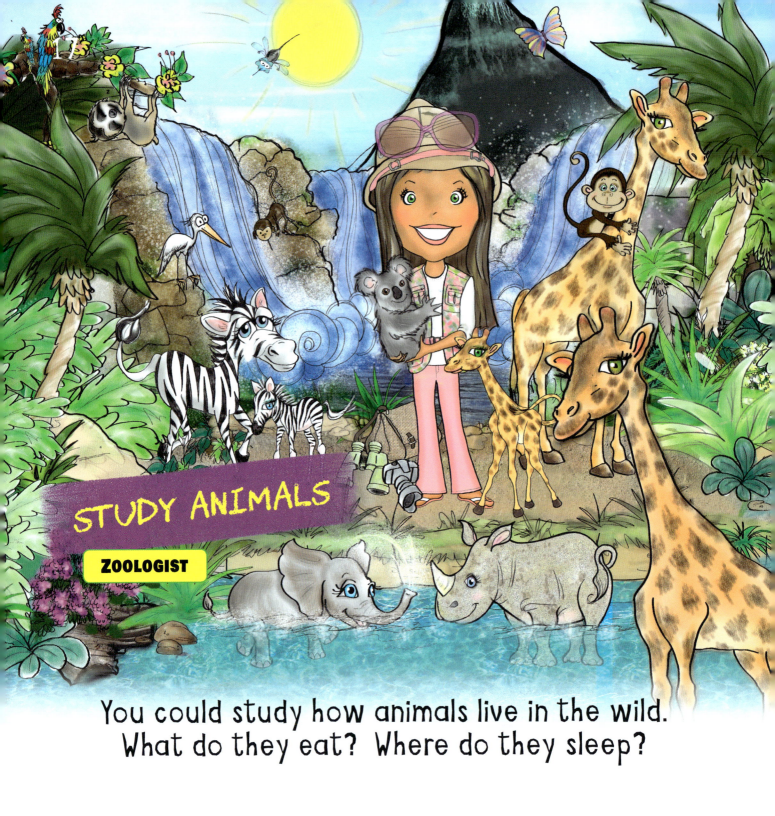

STUDY ANIMALS

ZOOLOGIST

You could study how animals live in the wild.
What do they eat? Where do they sleep?

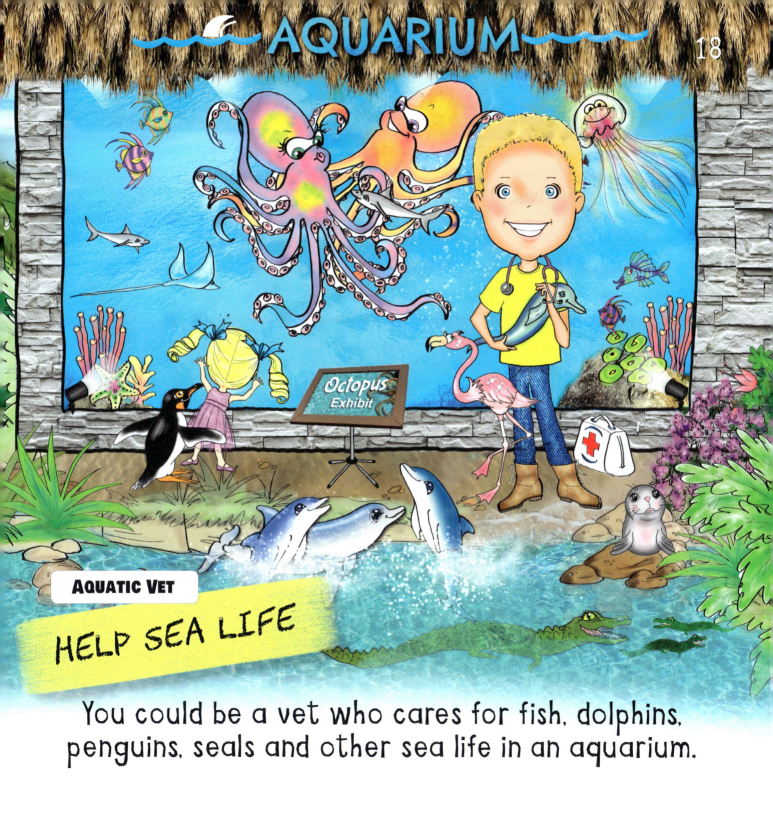

AQUATIC VET

HELP SEA LIFE

You could be a vet who cares for fish, dolphins, penguins, seals and other sea life in an aquarium.

You could be an airline pilot who flies jets around the world. Where would you fly your plane?

FLY JETS

AIRLINE PILOT

You could build robotic toys that walk and run.
What kind of robot would you build?
A dancing alien robot?
A robot pony?

MAKE ROBOTS

ROBOTICS ENGINEER

DESIGN SPACECRAFT

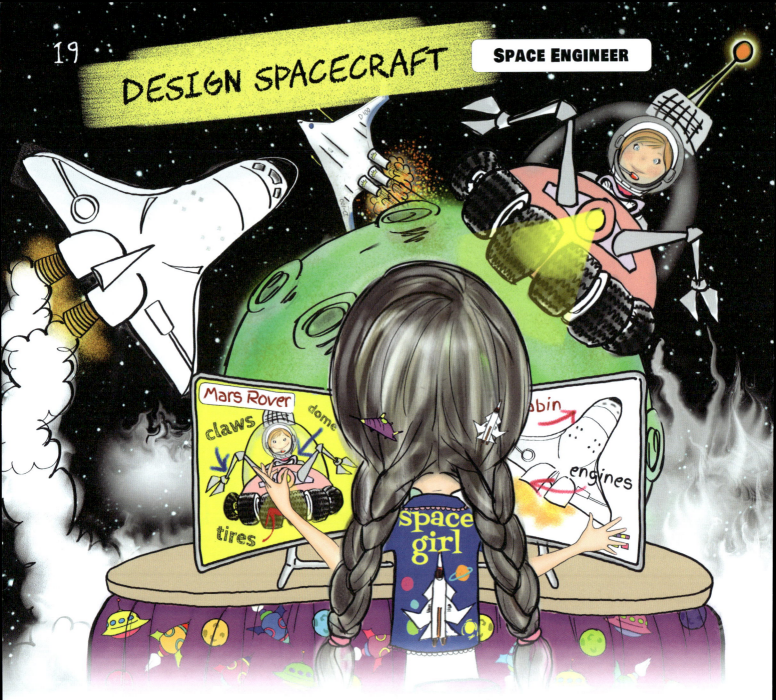

You could make spacecraft that zoom into space or rovers that explore other planets.

STUDY SPACE

ASTRONOMER

You could use telescopes to study space. If you discover a new planet, you get to name it! What else could be out in space?

You could create rides for fun parks. Would you make your roller coaster flip upside down?

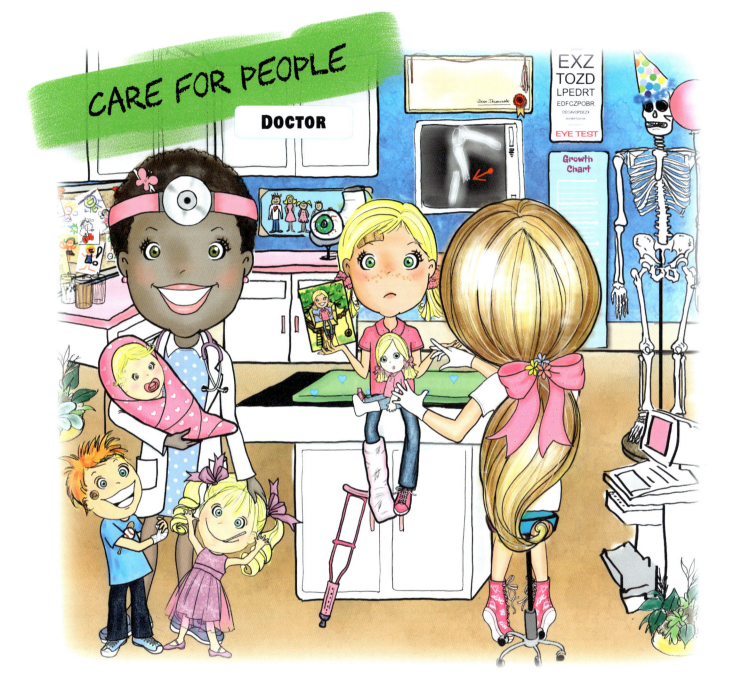

You could be a doctor who helps babies and children stay healthy and happy.

22

You could plan exhibits at museums. What creatures would you show?

LEAD THE COUNTRY

PRESIDENT

You could even be elected President!

Choosing what you will be
when you grow up is very special.

You have lots of time
to think, dream and plan.

Explore

Whatever you want to be,
always remember...

27

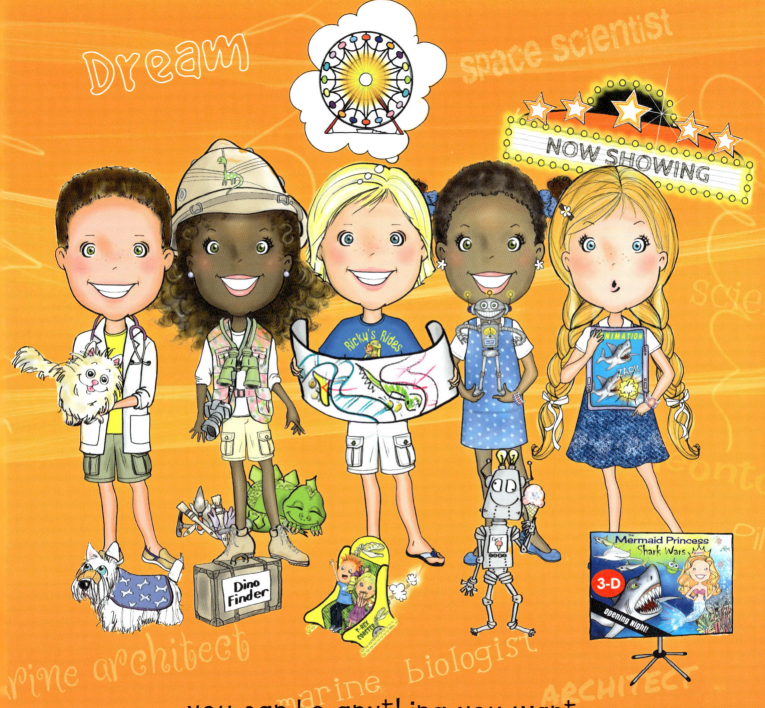

Dream

... you can be anything you want...

...so dream big...

...and chase your dream!

YOU
CAN BE
ANYTHING
YOU
DREAM!

What could YOU be?

MY FAVORITE IDEAS

This book belongs to

_____.

Some of the things I
might like to be are...

_____

_____

_____

_____

DREAM IT * PLAN IT * CHASE IT * BE IT!

NEXT STEPS

1) Think about what you could be

2) Explore career ideas

3) Learn more about the ones you like

4) Dream big (because you can be anything)

5) Believe in yourself

6) Chase your dreams!

7) Work hard to make them happen

Cut-out page for readers »

WHAT I WILL BE IS UP TO ME.

DREAM IT * PLAN IT * CHASE IT * BE IT!

WHAT IS YOUR FAVORITE CAREER?

Dear parents, I am keeping track of which future careers little readers like the most. You are invited to post a picture of your child's favorite career page. Just post a review on the book's page on Amazon and upload your snapshot.

IF YOU LIKED THIS BOOK,
PLEASE POST A REVIEW.

Thank you!

the author

Printed in Great Britain
by Amazon